INTERMEDIATE   LOW VOICE

Selected and edited by Nicola-Jane Kemp
and Heidi Pegler

CONTENTS

FABER ƒƒ MUSIC

HOW TO USE THIS BOOK

The Language of Song series was devised especially for the student singer as an introduction to a wealth of classical song repertoire, and to give them the tools and confidence required to sing in the primary mainland European languages. For this reason, no sung English translations are provided. The songs have been carefully chosen for their appropriateness of text and vocal range for the young student singer.

Preface to each song

Each song or aria is prefaced by a page of notes, containing: a brief background (setting it in its historical context or, where appropriate, its place in the drama); an idiomatic translation; and a phonetic pronunciation of the text. Any further notes at the bottom of each page highlight particular language points that may arise in the individual texts.

Translations: There are two translations for each song or aria. The first is a word-for-word translation directly underneath the text in the musical score. This is to enable the student to see exactly which words will be important for emphasis and interpretation. In addition, the prefatory page to each song includes an idiomatic translation, which will clarify the meaning of the text in grammatical English.

Phonetic pronunciation: A phonetic pronunciation of the original language, using the International Phonetic Alphabet (IPA), is provided for each song. A key to pronunciation is provided for each language at the back of this book and includes both examples from the song texts together with the closest English equivalents to the sounds explained. IPA symbols are given in these guides and careful study of these pages will be required in order to fully understand the IPA symbols that accompany the text for each song or aria. These are some of the basic principles that will help the singer to work along the right lines until they are able to refine pronunciation further with the help of a specialist language coach.

The accompanying CD

The CD provides the text for each song or aria spoken by the language consultants, all of whom are native speakers and work regularly with professional singers (see Biographies on pages 2 and 3). The speakers have attempted to make the text as clear as possible whilst maintaining the overall flow and dramatic content of the language. It is recommended that the language texts are prepared independently from the musical melody at first, as follows:

- Read the pronunciation key for the relevant language.
- Listen to the text on the CD, following the IPA guide for the song.
- Practise speaking the text slowly and clearly.
- When confident, slowly speak the text in the rhythm of the music.
- Gradually increase your speed to match the speed of the song.
- Additionally, practise delivering the text as a dramatic recitation showing your understanding of the language.

The CD also includes backing accompaniments for each song or aria. It should be remembered that these are a practice aid only and should not be substituted for a live accompaniment in performance.

Wherever possible, every effort has been made to return to the original source material. New accompaniments have been arranged for the Arie Antique and some (optional) ornamentation suggested, which appears in small staff notation above the vocal line. Editorial additions, such as dynamics, appear in square brackets.

EDITORS/CONSULTANTS: BIOGRAPHIES

Nicola-Jane Kemp

Nicola-Jane is an examiner for the Associated Board of the Royal Schools of Music and teaches voice to choral scholars at Clare College, Cambridge and St Paul's Girls' School, Hammersmith, London. She is also a professional singer, specialising in the coloratura repertoire (her signature role is 'Queen of the Night'), and works for companies as diverse as Music Theatre Wales and the Festival d'Aix-en-Provence, France. She has been broadcast on BBC Radio and her concert work takes her all round the UK – including the South Bank, Barbican, St Martin-in-the-Fields and St John's Smith Square in London – and to the Middle East.

Heidi Pegler

Heidi is Head of Singing at St Paul's Girls' School, where she runs a lively and busy singing department. She is an examiner for the Associated Board of the Royal Schools of Music and was a contributor on both *A Common Approach 2002* and *All Together!* – a book focusing on teaching music in groups (ABRSM). As a professional singer, she specialises in Baroque music (her debut solo CD, *Hark! The echoing air*, features Baroque music for Soprano, Trumpet and Orchestra) and has performed at many of Britain's leading venues including the Royal Albert Hall, Liverpool Philharmonic Hall, Bridgewater Hall, St David's Hall and the Royal Concert Hall, Glasgow.

Tina Ruta (Italian Consultant)

Born in Naples, Tina studied there at the Conservatoire San Pietro a Maiella and continued with Mark Raphael and Herbert-Caesari in England. She has sung in opera and recitals in England, France and Italy, and performed in West End theatre and at Glyndebourne. She has since gone on to develop a highly sought-after practice as an Italian language coach and has taught at the Guildhall School of Music and Drama and Trinity College of Music, both of which awarded her fellowships. She has coached singers for all the major European opera houses (including Covent Garden, Le Châtelet, Opera-Bastille, Berlin State Opera and Vienna State Opera) and has collaborated with many conductors including Giulini, Muti, Sinopoli, Colin Davis, Myung Whun Chung and Pappano. She also translates film scripts, librettos and lyrics.

Franziska Roth (German Consultant)

Franziska was born and grew up in Germany. She studied musicology at Salzburg University and continued her studies in piano and singing at the 'Mozarteum' Academy of Music. She has worked as a language coach for opera productions at Covent Garden, Glyndebourne, Le Châtelet and Opera-Bastille in Paris; festivals in Aix-en-Provence and Salzburg; and for staged projects in the Carnegie Hall, New York. She is highly sought after by many of the world's leading singers as a Lieder and oratorio coach, and has worked for many great conductors including Barenboim, Rattle, Solti, Haitink, Ghergiev, Pappano, Gardiner and Theilemann. She has been a member of the teaching staff at the Royal College of Music, London since 1989.

Michel Vallat (French Consultant)

Michel Vallat was born in France. He studied at the Sorbonne in Paris, where he graduated with a degree in Philosophy and at the Conservatoire National Superieur de Musique de Paris, where he won both the *Premier Prix de*

chant and the *Premier Prix d'Art lyrique*. He was appointed as a French coach at the Royal College of Music and as a Professor of Singing at the Guildhall School of Music and Drama, London. Michel works regularly with the Welsh National Opera, the Scottish Opera, the Glyndebourne Festival and the Royal Opera House (Covent Garden), and with singers such as Valerie Masterson, Della Jones, Thomas Hampson, Sergei Leiferkus, Bruce Ford, Renée Fleming, David Daniels, Sally Matthews, Joseph Calleja, Angelika Kirchschlager and Christopher Maltman.

Ramón Izeta (Spanish Consultant)

Born and brought up in Spain, Ramón was a member of a Basque Folklore Dance Group (Erkedz) for nearly twenty years, during which time the Group performed in Italy, Poland, the former Yugoslavia and France on international tours. He is trilingual, speaking Basque, Spanish and English, and has taught the Basque language in Spain. Since making his home in England, Ramón has taught both Basque and Spanish to private pupils. He has a great interest in music and, in collaboration with the pianist and vocal coach Stephen Wilder, Ramón has worked as a Spanish Coach for Classical Spanish Song at the Birmingham Conservatoire of Music.

© 2009 by Faber Music Ltd
First published in 2006 by Faber Music Ltd
This corrected edition first published in 2009
Bloomsbury House 74–77 Great Russell Street London WC1B 3DA
Cover design by Økvik Design
Music processed by MusicSet 2000
Printed in England by Caligraving Ltd
All rights reserved

ISBN10: 0-571-52344-7
EAN13: 978-0-571-52344-3

To buy Faber Music publications or to find out about the full range of titles available
please contact your local music retailer or Faber Music sales enquiries:

Faber Music Limited, Burnt Mill, Elizabeth Way, Harlow, CM20 2HX England
Tel: +44 (0)1279 82 89 82   Fax: +44 (0)1279 82 89 83
sales@fabermusic.com   fabermusic.com

CD recorded in Rectory Studio, High Wycombe, August 2005–May 2006
Piano: John Lenehan; Language consultants: Tina Ruta, Franziska Roth, Michel Vallat, Ramón Izeta
Recorded by John Lenehan; Produced by Nicola-Jane Kemp & Heidi Pegler
℗ 2006 Faber Music Ltd © 2006 Faber Music Ltd

Tu lo sai

You know it   **Giuseppe Torelli (1658–1709)**

Background

Born in Verona, Torelli was a composer and virtuoso string player. He studied composition with Giacomo Antonio Perti (1661–1756) and played both viola and violin during his career with the *Cappella musicale* at the church of San Petronio in Bologna. Torelli is primarily recognised for developing the solo concerto and concerto grosso, and for his compositions for strings and trumpet. He is believed to be the composer of this song although little is known of its origin. The original manuscript is lost and this version was part of a collection *Bel Canto* edited by Albert Fuchs (*c.*1901). The poet is reminding his love, saying 'Remember that I did love you'.

Idiomatic translation

You know how much I loved you,
you know it, you know it, cruel one!
I need no other reward
but that you think of me,
and then scorn an unfaithful one!

Pronunciation – **Tu lo sai** [tu lo sai]

Tu lo sai quanto t'amai,
tu lo sai kwanto tamai

Tu lo sai, lo sai, crudel!
tu lo sai lo sai krudel

Io non bramo altra mercé,
io non bramo altra mertʃe

Ma ricordati di me,
ma rikordati di me

E poi sprezza un infedel.
e poi spret:sa un infedel

Further notes

We suggest that each vowel in the word **Io** is roughly a quaver/eighth note in length. In the words **sai** and **amai**, **a** is the stressed vowel and **i** should be phrased off tastefully at the end of the note, especially in bar 44. Otherwise the two syllables are given separate notes – as indicated in the music.

① spoken text
② piano accompaniment

Tu lo sai

You know it

Poet unknown

Giuseppe Torelli (1658–1709)
Edited by Albert Fuchs

Original key not known
(First publ. in D♭ major)

Recording cue

Tu lo___ sai quan-to t'a-ma-i, Tu lo___
You it know how-much you I-loved, You it

sai, lo sai, cru - del!___ Io non bra - mo al - tra mer - cé,
know, it know, cruel-one! I (do) not desire other reward,

Ma ri - cor - da - ti di me, E poi sprez - za
but remember-yourself of me, and then scorn

un in - fe - del, e poi sprez - za un in - fe - del!
an unfaithful-one, and then scorn an unfaithful-one!

Toglietemi la vita ancor

Take my life also Alessandro Scarlatti (1660–1725)

Background

'Toglietemi la vita ancor' is taken from *Pompeo* (1683) – one of Scarlatti's early operas, also known for the familiar air 'O cessate di piagarmi'. After a performance of *Pompeo* in Naples in 1684 Scarlatti was appointed *Maestro di cappella* to Marquis del Carpio, the viceroy of Naples. Scarlatti is considered to be the founder of the Neapolitan school of 18th-century opera and was one of the first opera composers to make a distinction between the singing styles of aria and recitative. *Pompeo* is set in the period *c.*65 B. C. General 'Pompey the Great' has conquered the land of Pontus, captured its queen and brought her to Rome. At this point in the opera the queen's husband and former king of Pontus, Mitridate, has come to Rome to search for her. He is not able to find her and, believing her eternally lost to him, sings this aria in deep despair.

Idiomatic translation

VERSE 1
Cruel heavens:
if you wish to steal my heart,
take my life also.

VERSE 2
Harsh stars:
if you are glad about my sadness,
deny me the light of day.

Pronunciation – Toglietemi la vita ancor [tɔʎetɛmi la viˌtankɔr]

VERSE 1

Toglietemi la vita‿ancor,
tɔʎetɛmi   la viˌtankɔr

crudeli cieli,
krudeli tʃeli

se mi volete rapir il cor.
se mi volete rapir il kɔr

VERSE 2

Negatemi i rai del dì,
negatemi i rai dɛl di

severe sfere,
severe sfɛre

se vaghe siete del mio dolor.
se vage siete dɛl miɔ dolɔr

Further notes

Negatemi i needs to be sung with a slight separation for clarity, though avoid a full glottal stop.

spoken text

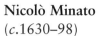 *piano accompaniment*

Toglietemi la vita ancor
Take my life also

Nicolò Minato
(*c.*1630–98)

Alessandro Scarlatti
(1660–1725)

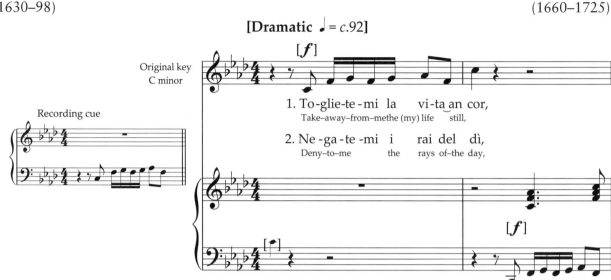

Amarilli, mia bella

Amaryllis, my beautiful one   Giulio Caccini (*c.*1545–1618)

Background

Caccini was a tenor singer and lutenist employed by the Medici family. A member of the *Camerata Fiorentina*, a group of intellectuals and musicians, Caccini developed a style of singing that would ultimately be known as *Bel Canto*. He published *Le Nuove Musiche* – a historically important volume of songs for solo voice and basso-continuo accompaniment – with a prefacing essay outlining his principles. This new style, known as 'monody', aimed to express the text in a direct manner having the melody closely following the words and using vocal ornamentation and embellishment to heighten emotional intensity. *Amarilli, mia bella* is uncharacteristically free of longer melismas and less chromatic compared to others in the collection. Caccini referred to this piece as a madrigal as its style is closer to recitative than to the pattern of regular strophic verses and phrase-lengths that would have been typical of an 'aria' at that time.

Idiomatic translation

Amaryllis, my beautiful one,
do you not believe, oh my heart's sweet desire,
that you are my love?
Believe it nevertheless, and if you still fear,
take this arrow of mine,
open my breast and you will see written on my heart:
Amaryllis is my love.

Pronunciation – Amarilli, mia bella [amaril:li mia bɛl:la]

Amarilli, mia bella,
amaril:li mia bɛl:la

non credi, o del mio cor dolce desio,
nɔn kredio dɛl mio kɔr dɔltʃe dezio

d'esser tu l'amor mio?
dɛs:ser tu lamor mio

Credilo pur, e se timor t'assale,
kredilɔ pur e se timor tas:sale

prendi questo mio strale,
prɛndi kwesto mio strale

aprimi il petto
aprimil pɛt:to

e vedrai scritto in core:
e vedrai skrit:toin kɔre

Amarilli è il mio amore.
amaril:li ɛil mioamore

Further notes

Check the liaisons carefully, which are clearly marked in the guide and in the musical score.

spoken text

piano accompaniment

Amarilli, mia bella

Amaryllis, my beautiful one

Giulio Caccini
(*c.*1545–1618)

Se tu m'ami

If you love me   attr. Alessandro Parisotti (1853–1913)

Background

Paolo Rolli's original poem (published in 1727) was set to music and appeared in the anthology *Arie Antiche Vol. 1*, edited by Alessandro Parisotti and published by Ricordi in 1885. In this collection, *Se tu m'ami* was attributed to Giovanni Pergolesi but, as an original source has never been found, modern scholars now believe that Alessandro Parisotti composed it himself. Whatever the truth of the matter, this song has remained widely popular. The singer is saying that though she loves her gentle shepherd, she also loves other men too.

Idiomatic translation

If you love me, if you sigh only for me, kind shepherd:
I am saddened by your suffering; I am delighted by your love.
But if you think that I should only love you in return,
little shepherd, you deceive yourself too easily.
Silvio chooses a beautiful red rose today;
but tomorrow he will hate it with the excuse that the thorns prick.
I myself, will not follow the advice of men.
Just because the lily pleases me doesn't mean I will despise the other flowers.

Pronunciation – Se tu m'ami [se tu mami]

Se tu m'ami, se tu sospiri
se tu mami   se tu sospiri

sol per me, gentil pastor,
sol per me dʒentil pastor

ho dolor de' tuoi martiri,
ɔ dolor de twoi martiri

ho diletto del tuo amor.
ɔ dilɛt:to dɛl tuoamor

Ma se pensi che soletto
ma se pɛnsi ke solɛt:to

io ti debba riamar,
iɔ ti dɛb:ba riamar

pastorello, sei soggetto
pastorɛl:lo sei sod:ʒɛt:to

facilmente a t'ingannar.
fatʃilmɛntea tingan:nar

Bella rosa porporina
bɛl:la rɔza porporina

oggi Silvio sceglierà,
ɔd:ʒi silviɔ ʃeʎera

con la scusa della spina
kɔn la skuza dɛl:la spina

doman poi la sprezzerà.
dɔman pɔi la sprɛt:sera

Ma degli uomini il consiglio
ma deʎiwɔminil   kɔnsiʎɔ

io per me non seguirò.
iɔ per me nɔn sɛgwirɔ

Non perchè mi piace il giglio
nɔn pɛrke mi pjatʃeil dʒiʎɔ

gli altri fiori sprezzerò.
ʎialtri fjɔri sprɛt:serɔ

Further notes

Do look carefully at the liaisons in bars 39–46, as they need to be negotiated smoothly and neatly. Emphasising the double consonants is particularly important in helping to characterise this song. Take care in the word **ingannar** that all the **n**'s are pronounced in the forward manner and that the English 'ng' sound is avoided. (See *Key to International Phonetic Alphabet*, page 76)

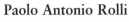

Se tu m'ami
If you love me

Paolo Antonio Rolli
(1687–1765)

attr. Alessandro Parisotti
(1853–1913)

Vaga luna

Lovely moon   Vincenzo Bellini (1801–35)

Background

Bellini's musical talent was recognised early on, with his first composition being written at just six years old. In his short life, he went on to become one of the most important 19th-century Romantic opera composers and was a master of the *Bel Canto* style. Widely remembered for the operas *Norma*, *Capuleti e I Montecchi*, and *I Puritani* (three of the greatest works in the repertoire), Bellini also wrote a number of pieces for voice and piano. Published in 1938 as *Composizioni da camera per canto e pianoforte*, these songs essentially bring his operatic style to the intimacy of the private drawing room and convey heartfelt emotion, tinged with melancholy. *Vaga luna* is one of three songs (*Tre Ariette* for mezzo-soprano and piano) based on an anonymous text. In true *Bel Canto* style, the singer must express all emotion and tonal beauty through the melody alone, with minimal accompaniment.

Idiomatic translation

VERSE 1

Lovely moon your silvery light
touches these banks and flowers,
and breathes the language of love
to the elements;
you are the only witness
of my fervent desire,
and can recount my throbbing heart
and sighs to my beloved.

VERSE 2

Tell her too, that distance
cannot soothe my grief,
that if I nurture a hope,
it is only for the future.
Tell her too, that day and night
I count the hours of sorrow,
that one promising hope
comforts me in my love.

Pronunciation – Vaga luna [va̲ga lu̲na]

VERSE 1

Vaga luna, che inargenti
va̲ga lu̲na ke̲ inardʒe̲nti

Queste rive e questi fiori
kwe̲ste ri̲ve   kwe̲sti fjo̲ri

Ed inspiri agli elementi
ɛd inspiriaʎie̲leme̲nti

Il linguaggio dell'amor;
il lingwa̲d:ʒo de̲l:lamo̲r

Testimonio or sei tu sola
tɛstimo̲njor   se̲i tu so̲la

Del mio fervido desir,
dɛl mi̲o fɛ̲rvido dɛzi̲r

Ed a lei che m'innamora
ɛd a le̲i ke min:namo̲ra

Conta i palpiti, i palpiti e i sospir.
ko̲ntai̲ palpiti i pa̲lpitje̲i sospi̲r

VERSE 2

Dille pur che lontananza
di̲l:le pu̲r ke lontana̲ntsa

Il mio duol non può lenir,
il mi̲ɔ dwo̲l nɔn pwo̲ lɛni̲r

Che se nutro una speranza,
ke   se nu̲trɔu̲na   spera̲ntsa

Ella è sol (si) nell'avvenir.
e̲l:laɛ sol (si) ne̲l:lav:vɛni̲r

Dille pur che giorno e sera
di̲l:le pur ke̲ dʒo̲rno e se̲ra

Conto l'ore del dolor,
kɔ̲nto lo̲re dɛl dolo̲r

Che una speme lusinghiera
ke̲una   spe̲me luzingje̲ra

Mi conforta nell'amor.
mi kɔnfɔ̲rta ne̲l:lamo̲r

Further notes

Check the pronunciation guide carefully for all the liaised words to make sure that the correct vowels are stressed – particularly the phrase **Ed inspiri agli elementi**. In the word **linguaggio** take care to pronounce the **n** carefully. In Italian 'lyric' diction, it is better to avoid the English 'ng' sound in this word and pronounce the **n** further forward (see *Key to International Phonetic Alphabet*, page 76). The accents in bars 24–26 and 50–52 should not be marked with heavy consonants but emphasised by stressing the vowels more expressively.

Vaga luna

Lovely moon

Vincenzo Bellini
(1801–35)

Andante cantabile [♩ = *c*.80]

Va-ga lu - na,_ che i-nar - gen - ti Que-ste
Lovely moon, that silvers these

Dil-le pur che_ lon-ta-nan - za Il mio
Say–to–her also that distance it my

ri - ve e_ que - sti fio - ri Ed in-spi-ri ed in-spi-ri a-gli e-le-
banks and these flowers and you–inhale, and you–inhale to–the elements

duol non può le - nir,_____ Che se nu - tro, se nu-tro u-na spe-
grief no longer soothes, that if I–nurture, if I–nurture a hope,

An Chloë

To Chloe

Wolfgang Amadeus Mozart (1756–91) K.524

Background

In terms of vocal output, Mozart is primarily remembered for his great operas and choral church music; however, he also composed around thirty songs. Although the songs are written on an intimate scale (as they were mostly intended for private performance) some are remarkable miniature dramas in themselves. This song, a setting of a text by Johann Georg Jacobi (1740–1814), was composed in Vienna in 1787. Effectively a pastoral seduction, the poet rhapsodises about the charms of the shepherdess Chloe.

Idiomatic translation

VERSE 1

When love looks out of your blue, bright, open eyes, my heart throbs and glows for the joy of looking into them; and I hold you and kiss your rosy, warm cheeks, dear girl; and trembling, I enclose you in my arms.

VERSE 2

Girl, girl, I clasp you tightly to my breast, only at the final moment, dying, will I let you go; then my euphoric feeling is over-shadowed by a dark cloud, and so I sit exhausted, though blissful, at your side.

Pronunciation – An Chloë [ˌan kloːe]

VERSE 1

Wenn die Lieb' aus deinen blauen,
vɛn diː liːp ˈaus daɪnən blaʊən

hellen, offnen Augen sieht,
hɛlən ˈɔfnən ˈaugən ziːt

und vor Lust hinein zu schauen
ʊnt foːɐ lʊst hɪnaɪn tsuː ʃauən

mir's im Herzen klopft und glüht;
miːɐs ɪm hɛrtsən klɔpft ʊnt glyːt

und ich halte dich und küsse
ʊnt ɪç haltə dɪç ʊnt kysə

deine Rosenwangen warm,
daɪnə roːzənvaŋən varm

liebes Mädchen, und ich schließe
liːbəs mɛːtçən ʊnt ɪç ʃliːsə

zitternd dich in meinen Arm!
tsɪtərnt dɪç ɪn maɪnən ˈaːrm

VERSE 2

Mädchen, Mädchen, und ich drücke
mɛːtçən mɛːtçən ʊnt ɪç drʏkə

dich an meinen Busen fest,
dɪç an maɪnən buːzən fɛst

der im letzten Augenblicke sterbend,
deːɐ ɪm lɛtstən ˈaugənblɪkə ʃtɛrbənt

sterbend nur dich von sich läßt;
ʃtɛrbənt nuːɐ dɪx fɔn zɪç lɛst

den berauschten Blick umschattet
deːn bəraʊʃtən blɪk ˈʊmʃatət

eine düstre Wolke mir,
ˌaɪnə dyːstrə vɔlkə miːɐ

und ich sitze dann ermattet,
ʊnt ɪç zɪtsə dan ɛɐmatət

aber selig neben dir.
ˌaːbɐ zeːlɪç neːbən diːɐ

Further notes

Note the difference in the length of the vowels, particularly words such as **drücke** and **düstre**. The first is a short vowel and the second is lengthened (see also **küsse** and **glüht**).

An Chloë

To Chloe

Johann Georg Jacobi
(1740–1814)

Wolfgang Amadeus Mozart K. 524
(1756–91)

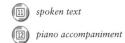

11 *spoken text*

12 *piano accompaniment*

Allegretto [♩ = 63]

Original key
E♭ major

Wenn die Lieb' aus dei-nen blau-en, hel-len,
When the love from your blue, bright,

off-nen Au-gen sieht,_ und vor Lust hin-ein zu schau-en,
open eyes looks, and for joy into (them) to look,

mir's_____ im Her-zen klopft_und_glüht; und ich hal-te dich und
to–me it in–the heart throbs and glows; and I hold you and

* Recording cue

Vergebliches Ständchen

Futile serenade　　　　　　　　Johannes Brahms (1833–97) Op. 84 No. 4

Background

Brahms took this poem from the Kretzschmer-Zuccalmaglio *Deutsche Volkslieder* (1840). An anonymous text, it was originally a folksong from the lower Rhine. Although Brahms composed this song as a duet, it is now more usually sung as a solo. The young suitor begs to be allowed into the house of his loved one but her mother has warned her about young men and she refuses to let him in. The musical direction *Lebhaft und gut gelaunt* (lively and good humoured) suggests that this might not be the end of the story!

Idiomatic translation

(He): Good evening, my precious, good evening, my pet! I come because I love you. Oh, open the door to me. Please open the door to me.

(She): My door is locked and I won't let you in. Mother gives me sound advice. If I were to allow you in, I would be finished!

(He): The night is so cold and the wind so icy that my heart will freeze and my love will die! Open up, my pet!

(She): If your love starts to die, then just let it go. If it keeps dying out, then go home to bed and rest. Good night, my boy!

Pronunciation – Vergebliches Ständchen [fɛɐɡeːplɪçəs ʃtɛntçən]

(Er) **Guten Abend, mein Schatz,**
　　　guːtən |aːbənt main ʃats

　　　guten Abend, mein Kind!
　　　guːtən |aːbənt main kɪnt

　　　Ich komm' aus Lieb' zu dir,
　　　|ɪç kɔm |aus liːp tsuː diːɐ

　　　ach, mach' mir auf die Tür,
　　　|ax max miːɐ |auf diː tyːr

　　　mach' mir auf die Tür!
　　　max miːɐ |auf diː tyːr

(Sie) **Mein' Tür ist verschlossen,**
　　　main tyːr |ist fɛɐʃlɔsən

　　　ich lass' dich nicht ein;
　　　|ɪç las dɪç nɪçt |ain

　　　Mutter, die rät mir klug,
　　　mʊtɐ diː rɛːt miːɐ kluːk

　　　wärst du herein mit Fug,
　　　vɛrst duː hɛrain mɪt fuːk

　　　wär's mit mir vorbei!
　　　vɛrs mɪt miːɐ foɐbai

(Er) **So kalt ist die Nacht,**
　　　zoː kalt |ɪst diː naxt

　　　so eisig der Wind,
　　　zoː |aizɪç deːɐ vɪnt

　　　dass mir das Herz erfriert,
　　　das miːɐ das hɛrts |ɛɐfriːɐt

　　　mein' Lieb' erlöschen wird;
　　　main liːp |ɛrlœʃən vɪrt

　　　öffne mir, mein Kind!
　　　|œfnə miːɐ main kɪnt

(Sie) **Löschet dein' Lieb';**
　　　lœʃət dain liːp

　　　lass' sie löschen nur!
　　　las ziː lœʃən nuːɐ

　　　Löschet sie immerzu,
　　　lœʃət ziː |ɪmɐtsuː

　　　geh' heim zu Bett, zur Ruh'!
　　　geː haim tsuː bɛt tsuːɐ ruː

　　　Gute Nacht, mein Knab'!
　　　guːtə naxt main knaːp

Further notes

There is much text to get through at speed here. The singer may like to practise speaking the last four bars of each stanza in particular to make sure that all the consonants are nimbly articulated.

13 *spoken text*
14 *piano accompaniment*

Vergebliches Ständchen

Futile serenade

Folksong from the lower Rhine

Johannes Brahms Op. 84 No. 4
(1833–97)

43 kalt ist die Nacht,_ so ei - sig der Wind,
cold is the night, so icy the wind,

p

48 so ei - sig der Wind, dass mir das Herz er - friert,
so icy the wind, that to-me the heart freezes,

53 mein' Lieb' er - lö - schen wird; öff - ne mir, mein Kind, öff - ne mir,
my love to-die-down will; open to-me, my pet, open to-me,

p

58 **Lebhafter** (*Livelier*)

öff - ne mir, öff - ne mir,_ mein Kind!
open to-me, open to-me, my pet!

f

Ständchen

Serenade   **Franz Peter Schubert (1797–1828) D.957 No. 4**

Background

Out of the ten poems by Ludwig Rellstab (1799–1860) that Schubert set to music, seven were included in the collection *Schwanengesang* ('Swan Song') published posthumously in 1829. *Ständchen* is one of them. Composed only a few weeks before his death in 1828, it is perhaps one of the most well-known serenades ever written. The staccato accompaniment, which evokes the intimacy of a lute or mandolin, and the flowing vocal line express the expectant passion of the lover on a beautiful summer's night.

Idiomatic translation

Softly, my songs plead through the night to you; down below, in the peaceful grove, sweetheart, come to me!
The slender tree-tops rustle and whisper in the moonlight; don't be afraid my fair one of anyone over-hearing and betraying us.
Do you hear the song of the nightingales? Ah, they plead to you; the notes of their sweet lament plead to you on my behalf.
They understand the heart's yearning and know the pain of love, touching each tender heart with their silvery notes.
Let your heart also be moved, sweetheart, hear me! Trembling, I await you.
Come, make me happy!

Pronunciation – Ständchen [ʃtɛntçən]

Leise flehen meine Lieder
laizə fleːən mainə liːdɐ

durch die Nacht zu dir;
dʊrç diː naxt tsuː diːɐ

In den stillen Hain hernieder,
|ɪn deːn ʃtɪlən hain herniːdɐ

Liebchen, komm zu mir!
liːpçən kɔm tsuː miːɐ

Flüsternd schlanke Wipfel rauschen
flʏstɛrnt ʃlaŋkə vɪpfəl rauʃən

in des Mondes Licht;
|ɪn dɛs moːndəs lɪçt

Des Verräters feindlich Lauschen
dɛs fɛreːtɐs faintlɪç lauʃən

fürchte, Holde, nicht.
fʏrçtə hɔldə nɪçt

Hörst die Nachtigallen schlagen?
høːrst diː naxtɪgalən ʃlaːgən

Ach! sie flehen dich,
|ax ziː fleːən dɪç

mit der Töne süßen Klagen
mɪt deːɐ tøːnə zyːsən klaːgən

flehen sie für mich.
fleːən ziː fyːɐ mɪç

Sie verstehn des Busens Sehnen,
ziː fɛɐʃteːn dɛs buːzəns zeːnən

kennen Liebesschmerz,
kɛnən liːbəsʃmerts

rühren mit den Silbertönen
ryːrən mɪt deːn zɪlbɐtøːnən

jedes weiche Herz.
jeːdəs vaiçə herts

Laß auch dir die Brust bewegen,
las |aux diːɐ diː brust bəveːgən

Liebchen, höre mich!
liːpçən høːrə mɪç

Bebend harr' ich dir entgegen!
beːbənt har |ɪç diːɐ |entgeːgən

Komm, beglücke mich!
kɔm bəglʏkə mɪç

Further notes

In words such as **flüsternd** and **durch**, the 'r' becomes difficult to pronounce at speed and becomes like the [ɐ] word endings [flʏstɛɐnt], [dʊɐç]. (See notes on *Mariä Wiegenlied* for help in the usual pronunciation of **durch**.)

Ständchen
Serenade

Ludwig Rellstab
(1799–1860)

Franz Schubert D. 957 No. 4
(1797–1828)

Lei - se fle - hen mei - ne Lie - der durch die Nacht zu dir;
Softly plead my songs through the night to you;

In den stil - len Hain her - nie - der,
In the quiet grove down-below,

Lieb - chen, komm zu mir!
sweetheart, come to me!

Flüs - ternd schlan - ke Wip - fel rau - schen in des Mon - des Licht,
Whisperingly slender tree-tops rustle in the moon's light,

Mariä Wiegenlied

Mary's lullaby　　　　　　　　　**Max Reger (1873–1916) Op. 76 No. 52**

Background

Born in Brand and educated in Weiden, the pianist and composer Max Reger is principally remembered for his organ music. He did, however, compose music for many genres during his prolific yet short life. Although influenced by both Brahms and Bach, his music is considered to have taken the German style from the nineteenth-century tradition firmly into the twentieth-century through his use of free modulation and contrapuntal textures. Composed in 1912, *Mariä Wiegenlied* has text by Martin Boelitz (1874–1918) and comes from the collection *Schlichte Weisen* ('Simple Melodies'). Although excommunicated from the Catholic Church on marrying a divorced, protestant woman, Reger used much religious thematic material in his works. This Virgin's lullaby is composed in a more straightforward musical language than his usual, contrapuntally complex musical style.

Idiomatic translation

Mary sits near the rose grove and cradles her child Jesus;
a warm summer breeze wafts gently through the leaves.
At her feet, a colourful little bird sings:
Sleep, little child, sweetly, go to sleep now!
Your smile is lovely, and your joyful slumber, even more lovely.
Lay your weary head firmly on your mother's breast!
Sleep, little child, sweetly, go to sleep now!

Pronunciation – **Mariä Wiegenlied** [mari̯ɛ viːɡənliːt]

Maria sitzt am Rosenhag und wiegt ihr Jesuskind,

mari̯a zɪtst |am roːzənhaːk |ʊnt viːkt |iːɐ jeːzʊskɪnt

durch die Blätter leise weht der warme Sommerwind.

dʊrç di: blɛtɐ laɪzə veːt deːɐ varmə zɔmɐvɪnt

Zu ihren Füßen singt ein buntes Vögelein:

tsu: |iːrən fyːsən zɪŋt |ain bʊntəs føːɡəlain

Schlaf', Kindlein, süße, schlaf' nun ein!

ʃlaːf kɪntlain zyːsə ʃlaːf nuːn |ain

Hold ist dein Lächeln, holder deines Schlummers Lust,

hɔlt |ist dain lɛçəln hɔldɐ dainəs ʃlʊmɐs lʊst

leg dein müdes Köpfchen fest an deiner Mutter Brust!

leːk dain myːdəs kœpfçən fɛst |an dainɐ mʊtɐ brʊst

Further notes

Do check that the **ch** [ç] sounds are correctly pronounced. They are all the same in this song. The word **durch** is problematic for English speakers. Practise saying [dʊr - ɪç], then leave out the [ɪ] – [dʊr - ç], then bring the two sounds closer together.

17 spoken text
18 piano accompaniment

Mariä Wiegenlied
Mary's lullaby

Martin Boelitz
(1874–1918)

Max Reger Op. 76 No. 52
(1873–1916)

Original key
F major

Allegretto [♩. = c.60] *p*

Ma - ri - a sitzt am Ro - sen - hag und wiegt ihr Je - sus - kind,
Mary sits by the rose-grove and cradles her Jesus–child,

durch die Blät - ter lei - se weht der war - me Som - mer - wind.
through the leaves softly wafts the warm summer-wind.

Zu ih - ren Fü - ßen singt ein bun - tes Vö - ge -lein:
At her feet sings a colourful little–bird:

Schlaf', Kind - lein, sü - - ße, schlaf'_____ nun
Sleep, little–child, sweetly, sleep now

una corda

Die Lotosblume

The lotus flower — Robert Alexander Schumann (1810–56) Op. 25 No. 7

Background

Die Lotosblume is part of the song-cycle *Myrthen, Liederkries* ('Myrtles, Song cycle'), which contains 26 songs Schumann composed in February 1840 as a wedding present for his beloved Clara Wieck. The pair were forcibly separated by Clara's father, who opposed their union, and the song-cycle expresses all the joys and pains of love and being apart. The text comes from a poem by Heinrich Heine (1797–1856), which conveys the idea of total worship between a man and a woman. It is one of several themes concerning relationships that Schumann explores throughout the whole cycle.

Idiomatic translation

The lotus flower is frightened by the sun's magnificence and lowering her head, dreamily awaits nightfall.
Her lover, the moon, wakes her with his light and kindly, she reveals her virtuous flower-face to him.
She blooms and glows and shines; and staring without words at the sky;
she wafts her sweet fragrance and weeps and trembles with love and love's pain.

Pronunciation – Die Lotosblume [di: loːtɔsbluːmə]

Die Lotosblume ängstigt
di: loːtɔsbluːmə |ɛŋstɪçt

sich vor der Sonne Pracht,
zɪç foːɐ deːɐ zɔnə praxt

und mit gesenktem Haupte
|ʊnt mɪt gəzɛŋktəm hauptə

erwartet sie träumend die Nacht.
ɛɐvaːrtət zi: trɔɪmənt di: naxt

Der Mond, der ist ihr Buhle,
deːɐ moːnt deːɐ |ɪst |iːɐ buːlə

er weckt sie mit seinem Licht,
|eːɐ vɛkt zi: mɪt zainəm lɪçt

und ihm entschleiert sie freundlich
|ʊnt |iːm |ɛntʃlaiɐt zi: frɔɪntlɪç

ihr frommes Blumengesicht.
|iːɐ frɔməs bluːməngəzɪçt

Sie blüht und glüht und leuchtet,
zi: blyːt |ʊnt glyːt |ʊnt lɔɪçtət

und starret stumm in die Höh';
|ʊnt ʃtarət ʃtʊm |ɪn di: høː

sie duftet und weinet und zittert
zi: duftət |ʊnt vainət |ʊnt tsɪtert

vor Liebe und Liebesweh.
foːɐ liːbə |ʊnt liːbesveː

Further notes

Do take care to understand the different 'u' sounds in this text. In particular the sentence **Sie blüht und glüht und leuchtet** will need special attention.

Die Lotosblume
The lotus flower

19 spoken text
20 piano accompaniment

Heinrich Heine
(1797–1856)

Robert Schumann Op. 25 No. 7
(1810–56)

Ziemlich langsam (*Fairly slow*) [♩ = 96]

Original key
F major

Die Lo - tos - blu - me äng - stigt
The lotus-flower worries

sich vor der Son - ne Pracht,
(herself) before the sun's magnificence,

und mit ge - senk - tem
and with bowed

Haup - te er - war - tet sie träu-mend die Nacht. Der
head awaits she dreamily the night. The

Mond, der ist __ ihr Buh - le, er weckt sie mit sei - nem Licht, und
moon, who is her lover, he wakes her with his light, and

Die Forelle

The Trout   Franz Peter Schubert (1797–1828) D.550/Op.32

Background

One of Schubert's best-loved songs, *Die Forelle* was composed *c*.1817 and the melody later formed the theme and variations of the fourth movement of his Piano Quintet in A major (D.667). This moral tale originally contained four extra verses of warning to young maidens but Schubert omitted these and turned what is often considered a second-rate poem into a masterpiece, with its attractive melody and playful virtuosity of the piano accompaniment.

Idiomatic translation

In a clear little brook, a capricious trout darted about happily, as swift as an arrow.
I stood upon the bank and watched, in sweet calm, the lively little fish swimming in the clear little brook.
An angler stood with his rod at the water's edge and coolly watched as the little fish twisted to and fro.
So long as the water remains clear, I thought, he would not be able to catch the fish with his fishing tackle.
But in the end, the poacher became impatient. He craftily muddied the little brook and before I realised it,
the rod jerked and the little fish was writhing on the end of it. I, with heated blood, could only look on at the cheated one.

Pronunciation – Die Forelle [di: fɔrɛ̠lə]

VERSE 1

In einem Bächlein helle,
|ɪn |ainəm bɛ̠çlain   hɛ̠lə

da schoß in froher Eil
da: ʃɔs |ɪn fro:ɐ̯ |ail

die launische Forelle
di: launɪʃə   fɔrɛ̠lə

vorüber wie ein Pfeil.
fory̠:bɐ   vi: |ain pfail

Ich stand an dem Gestade
|ɪç ʃtant |an de:m gəʃta:də

und sah in süßer Ruh
|ʊnt za: |ɪn zy:sɐ ru:

des muntern Fischleins Bade
des mʊntərn fɪʃlains   ba̠:də

im klaren Bächlein zu.
|ɪm kla̠:rən bɛ̠çlain   tsu:

VERSE 2

Ein Fischer mit der Rute
|ain fɪʃɐ   mɪt de:ɐ̯ ru̠:tə

wohl an dem Ufer stand,
vo:l |an de:m |u̠:fɐ ʃtant

und sah's mit kaltem Blute,
|ʊnt za:s mɪt ka̠ltəm blu̠:tə

wie sich das Fischlein wand.
vi: zɪç das fɪʃlain   vant

So lang' dem Wasser Helle,
zo: laŋ de:m va̠sɐ   hɛ̠lə

so dacht ich, nicht gebricht,
zo: daxt |ɪç nɪçt gəbrɪ̠çt

so fängt er   die Forelle
zo: fɛŋt |e:ɐ̯ di: fɔrɛ̠lə

mit seiner Angel nicht.
mɪt za̠inɐ |aŋəl   nɪçt

VERSE 3

Doch endlich ward dem Diebe
dɔx |ɛntlɪç vart de:m di̠:bə

die Zeit zu lang.
di: tsa̠it tsu: laŋ

Er macht das Bächlein tückisch trübe,
|e:ɐ̯ maxt das bɛ̠çlain ty̠kɪʃ   try̠:bə

und eh ich es gedacht,
|ʊnt |e: |ɪç |es gəda̠xt

so zuckte seine Rute,
zo: tsʊ̠ktə za̠inə ru̠:tə

das Fischlein zappelt dran,
das fɪʃlain   tsa̠pəlt dran

und ich mit regem Blute
|ʊnt |ɪç mɪt re̠:gəm blu̠:tə

sah die Betrogne an.
za: di: bətro̠:gnə |an

Further notes

There is plenty of scope for dramatising this little scene and the singer must be particularly fluent in speaking the text with lively articulation – especially the phrase **und eh ich es gedacht**. There are some lovely onomatopoeic words to enjoy (**tückisch/zuckte/zappelt** etc.).

44

Die Forelle
The Trout

Christian Friedrich Daniel Schubart
(1739–91)

Franz Schubert D. 550 Op. 32
(1797–1828)

Etwas lebhaft *(Somewhat lively)* [♩ = 84]

Original key
D♭ major

1. In ei - nem Bäch -lein hel - le, da
   In a little–brook clear, there

(2.) Fi - scher mit der Ru - te wohl
    fisherman with the rod indeed

schoß in fro - her Eil die lau - ni - sche Fo - rel - le vor-
shot in happy haste the moody trout past–by

an dem U - fer_ stand, und sah's mit kal - tem Blu - te, wie
on the shore stood, and watched it with cold blood, how

Le charme

The charm   **Ernest Amédée Chausson (1855–99) Op. 2 No. 2**

Background

Ernest Chausson (having previously studied law) went to the Paris Conservatoire to study composition under Jules Massenet at the unusually late age of twenty-five. He stayed at the Conservatoire only a short time, however, before leaving to study privately with César Franck. Tragically killed in a bicycle accident aged only forty-four, Chausson wrote thirty-four songs in total. *Le charme* is one of the earliest, written in 1879 while Chausson was still studying with Massenet, and is set to text by Armand Silvestre (1837–1901). Massenet, an admirer of Silvestre, may have influenced Chausson's choice, though this was the only text by the poet that he set. There is a simple, touching quality about this song that expresses the poem with great clarity.

Idiomatic translation

VERSE 1
When your smile surprised me,
I felt my entire being tremble,
But what had subdued my spirit
I couldn't recognize at first.

VERSE 2
When your glance fell on me,
I felt my soul melt into itself,
But what this turmoil was
I could not at first describe it.

VERSE 3
What vanquished me forever
Was a more sorrowful charm,
And I knew that I loved you
only when seeing your first tear.

Pronunciation – Le charme [lə ʃaʀmə]

VERSE 1

Quand ton sourire me surprit,
kɑ̃   tõ   suʀiɾə mə syʀpʀi

Je sentis frémir tout mon‿être,
ʒə sɑ̃ti   fʀemir tu   mõ(n)ɛtɾə

Mais ce qui domptais mon‿esprit
mɛ   sə ki dõtɛ   mõ(n)ɛspʀi

Je ne pus d'abord le connaître.
ʒə nə py dabɔr   lə kɔnɛtɾə

VERSE 2

Quand ton regard tomba sur moi,
kɑ̃   tõ   ʀəgaʀ tõba syʀ mwa

Je sentis mon‿âme se fondre,
ʒə sɑ̃ti   mõ(n)ɑmə sə fõdʀə

Mais ce que serait cet‿émoi,
mɛ   sə kə səʀɛ   sɛ(t)emwa

Je ne pus d'abord en répondre.
ʒə nə py dabɔr   ɑ̃ ʀepõdʀə

VERSE 3

Ce qui me vainquit‿à jamais,
sə ki mə vɛ̃ki(t)a   ʒamɛ

Ce fut‿un plus douloureux charme,
sə fy(t)œ̃ ply dulurø   ʃaʀmə

Et je n'ai su que je t'aimais,
e ʒə ne sy kə ʒə tɛmɛ

Qu'en voyant ta première larme.
kɑ̃   vwajɑ̃ ta pʀəmjɛʀə laʀmə

Further notes

Note that the final 'd' in **d'abord** is not pronounced and the [ʀ] should not be liaised in verse two.

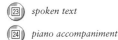

Le charme

The charm

Armand Silvestre
(1837–1901)

Ernest Chausson Op. 2 No. 2
(1855–99)

50

Le secret

The secret   Gabriel Urbain Fauré (1845–1924) Op. 23 No. 3

Background

Fauré's musical gifts were recognised as a child, when an elderly blind lady heard him playing the harmonium in the local chapel. He studied at L'École Niedermeyer in Paris, enabling him to mix with other composers and poets of the day, including Saint-Saëns. By the time he was twenty, he had published twenty songs. *Le secret* is a setting of a poem by Armand Silvestre (1837–1901) and was composed *c.*1881. It follows the poem's three-part structure: the secrecy of love at the dawn of morning; the height of love at midday; and love's disappearance with the setting of the evening sun. Dedicated to Alice Boissonnet, though it was first performed by a bass singer, it falls into the second of three collections published by Hamelle in 1897.

Idiomatic translation

VERSE 1

I wish that the morning may not be aware of the name that I told to the night,
and that in the dawn breeze, it may vanish soundlessly like a teardrop that evaporates.

VERSE 2

I wish that the day may proclaim the love that I have concealed from the morning,
and, inclining over my open heart, may set it alight like a grain of incense.

VERSE 3

I wish that sunset may forget the secret that I told to the day,
and bring it away with my love in the folds of its faded gown.

Pronunciation – Le secret [lə səkRɛ]

VERSE 1

Je veux que le matin l'ignore
ʒə vø kə lə matɛ̃ liɲɔRə

Le nom que j'ai dit | à la nuit,
lə nõ kə ʒe di a la nɥi

Et qu'au vent de l'aube, sans bruit,
e ko vã də lobə sã bRɥi

Comme_une larme_il s'évapore.
kɔ(m)ynə laR(m)il sevapɔRə

VERSE 2

Je veux que le jour le proclame
ʒə vø kə lə ʒuR lə pRɔklamə

L'amour qu'au matin j'ai caché,
lamuR ko matɛ̃ ʒe kaʃe

Et sur mon coeur_ouvert penché
e syR mõ kœ(R)uvɛR pãʃe

Comme_un grain d'encens, il l'enflamme.
kɔ(m)œ̃ gRɛ̃ dãsã ilãflamə

VERSE 3

Je veux que le couchant l'oublie
ʒə vø kə lə kuʃã lubliə

Le secret que j'ai dit | au jour,
lə səkRɛ kə je di o ʒuR

Et l'emporte_avec mon_amour,
e lãpɔR(t)avɛk mõ(n)amuR

Aux plis de sa robe pâlie!
o pli də sa Rɔbə paliə

Further notes

Do check the suggested liaisons carefully.

[25] *spoken text*
[26] *piano accompaniment*

Le secret
The secret

Armand Silvestre
(1837–1901)

Gabriel Fauré Op. 23 No. 3
(1845–1924)

Aurore

Dawn   Gabriel Urbain Fauré (1845–1924) Op. 39 No. 1

Background

With a text by Armand Silvestre (1837–1901), *Aurore* was composed by Fauré in 1884 and published by Hamelle in 1885. It was dedicated to Madame Henriette Roger-Jourdain, the daughter of the artist Henri Moulignon. She and her husband Joseph, also an artist, lived along the Boulevard Berthier and were frequent hosts and patrons of art in Paris in the 1880s. Madame Roger-Jourdain captured the imagination of those around her, inspiring musical compositions and portraits alike. One particular group of friends included Fauré and the painters John Singer-Sargent and Albert Besnard.

Idiomatic translation

VERSE 1

The stars fly away from the gardens of the night,
like golden bees attracted by an invisible honey;
and in the distance, dawn spreads out her blank canvas,
weaving the sky's blue mantle with silver threads.

VERSE 2

From the garden of my heart, intoxicated by a leisurely dream,
my desires fly away with the advancing steps of morning,
like a weightless swarm, called to the copper-coloured horizon
by an eternal, distant and plaintive song.

VERSE 3

They fly to your feet, stars chased out from the heavens,
exiled from the golden sky where your beauty blossoms,
and, searching unknown paths to reach you,
they mingle their dying brightness with the birth of day.

Pronunciation – Aurore [oʀɔ̯ʀ]

VERSE 1

Des jardins de la nuit s'envolent les̯ étoiles,
dε ʒaʀdɛ̃ də la nɥi sɑ̃vɔlə lε(z)etwa̯lə

Abeilles d'or qu'attire̯ un̯ invisible miel,
abɛjə dɔʀ kati̯(ʀ)œ̃(n)ɛ̃viziblə mjε̯l

Et l'aube, au loin tendant la candeur de ses toiles,
e lo(b)o lwɛ̃ tɑ̃dɑ̯̃ la kɑ̃dœʀ də sε twa̯lə

Trame de fils d'argent le manteau bleu du ciel.
tʀa̯mə də fil daʀʒɑ̃ lə mɑ̯̃to blø dy sjε̯l

VERSE 2

Du jardin de mon coeur qu'un rêve lent | enivre,
dy jaʀdɛ̃ də mõ kœʀ kœ̃ ʀεvə lɑ̃ ɑ̃ni̯vʀə

S'envolent mes désirs sur les pas du matin,
sɑ̃vɔ̯lə mε dezi̯ʀ syʀ lε pa dy matɛ̃

Comme̯ un̯ essaim léger qu'à l'horizon de cuivre,
kɔ(m)œ̃(n)esɛ̃ leʒe̯ ka lɔʀizõ̯ də kɥi̯vʀə

Appelle̯ un chant plaintif, éternel̯ et lointain.
apε(l)œ̃ ʃɑ̃ plɛ̃ti̯f etεʀnε(l)e lwɛ̃tɛ̃

VERSE 3

Ils volent̯ à tes pieds, astres chassés des nues,
il vɔlə(t)a tε pje̯ a̯stʀə ʃase̯ dε nyə̯

Exilés du ciel d'or̯ où fleurit ta beauté
εgzile dy sje̯l dɔ(ʀ)u flœʀi̯ ta bote̯

Et, cherchant jusqu'à toi des routes̯ inconnues,
e ʃεʀʃɑ̃ ʒyska twa dε ʀutə(z)ɛ̃kɔnyə̯

Mêlent̯ au jour naissant leur mourante clarté.
mε̯lə(t)o ʒuʀ nεsɑ̃ lœʀ muʀɑ̯̃tə klaʀte̯

Further notes

Please note that the final s is not pronounced in **fils**, which is the plural of 'fil' (thread), unlike 'fils', which means 'son'.

Aurore
Dawn

27 *spoken text*

28 *piano accompaniment*

Armand Silvestre
(1837–1901)

Gabriel Fauré Op. 39 No. 1
(1845–1924)

Original key
G major

Andante [♩ = 76–82]   *dolce*

Des jar-dins de la nuit s'en-vo-lent les é - toi - les,
From the gardens of the night fly away the stars,

pp

A - beil-les d'or qu'at -tire un in - vi - si - ble miel, ___ Et
bees of gold that attracts an invisible honey, and

poco a poco cresc.

f

l'au - be, au loin ten -dant la can-deur de ses toi - les, Tra - me de fils d'ar-
the dawn, in the distance stretching the candour of her canvasses, weaves with threads of

poco a poco cresc.

f

-gent le man-teau bleu du ___ ciel.
silver the mantle blue of the sky.

p

Clair de lune

Moonlight   Gabriel Urbain Fauré (1845–1924) Op. 46 No. 2

Background

Clair de lune was the first of several poems by the Symbolist poet, Paul Verlaine (1844–96) that Fauré set to music. Composed in 1887 and dedicated to Emmanuel Jadin, it is subtitled 'Menuet', a dance which is principally represented in the accompaniment. The poem comes from the collection *Fêtes galantes* ('Romantic festivities') inspired by the world of the *commedia dell'arte** and the atmospheric paintings of Watteau. Typical of symbolist poems, the text is full of unusual associations and images, sometimes selected more for the sounds of the words than their literal meaning. Rather than musically interpreting the sense of each phrase (unlike Debussy who was also inspired to set Verlaine's poems), Fauré prefers to capture the overall atmosphere of elegance, mystery and melancholy.

Idiomatic translation

VERSE 1

Your soul is a distinctive landscape
where charming maskers and bergamaskers go to and fro
playing the lute and dancing, and are almost
sad beneath their fantastical disguises.

VERSE 2

While singing in a minor key
of triumphant love and the propitious life,
they do not seem to believe in their good fortune,
and their song intertwines with the moonlight.

VERSE 3

In the calm moonlight, sad and beautiful,
which sets the birds in the trees a-dreaming
and the fountains sob with ecstasy,
the tall, slender fountains amongst the marble statues.

Pronunciation – Clair de lune [klɛʀ də lynə]

VERSE 1

Votre âme est un paysage choisi
vɔt(ʀ)a(m)ɛ(t)œ̃   peizaʒə ʃwazi

Que vont charmant masques et bergamasques,
kə võ ʃaʀmɑ̃   maskə(z)e bɛʀgamaskə

Jouant du luth et dansant, et quasi
ʒuɑ̃   dy ly(t)e dɑ̃sɑ̃   e kazi

Tristes sous leurs déguisements fantasques.
tʀistə su   lœʀ degizəmɑ̃   fɑ̃taskə

VERSE 2

Tout en chantant sur le mode mineur
tu(t)ɑ̃   ʃɑ̃tɑ̃   syʀ lə mɔdə minœʀ

L'amour vainqueur et la vie opportune,
lamuʀ   vɛ̃kœʀ   e la vi ɔpɔʀtynə

Ils n'ont pas l'air de croire à leur bonheur
il nõ   pa lɛʀ də kʀwa(ʀ)a lœʀ bɔnœʀ

Et leur chanson se mêle au clair de lune,
e lœʀ ʃɑ̃sõ   sə mɛ(l)o klɛʀ də lynə

VERSE 3

Au calme clair de lune triste et beau,
o   kalmə klɛʀ də lynə tʀis(t)e bo

Qui fait rêver les oiseaux dans les arbres
ki   fɛ ʀeve lɛ(z)wazo dɑ̃   lɛ(z)aʀbʀə

Et sangloter d'extase les jets d'eau,
e   sɑ̃glɔte   dɛkstazə lɛ ʒɛ   do

Les grands jets d'eau sveltes parmi les marbres.
lɛ   gʀɑ̃   ʒɛ do   svɛltə paʀmi lɛ maʀbʀə

Further notes

*The characters of the Italian comedy included Columbine, Pulcinella and Harlequin, who speak in the dialect of Bergamo – hence *bergamasque* (dance of Bergamo).

Clair de lune

Moonlight

Paul Verlaine
(1844–96)

Gabriel Fauré Op. 46 No. 2
(1845–1924)

spoken text

piano accompaniment

El majo discreto

*The discreet man**   Enrique Granados (1867–1916)

Background

Granados, a Catalonian composer and pianist, studied in Barcelona and Paris, and is principally known for his piano and vocal music. His piano suite *Goyesca* was made into an opera and performed at the Metropolitan Opera House in New York in 1916. Two months later, Granados and his wife left New York to return to Spain. The boat they were travelling on was torpedoed by the Germans and, although Granados made it onto a life raft, he saw his wife struggling in the water and leapt in to try and save her. Both tragically perished. 'El majo discreto' comes from *Colección de tonadillas escritas en estilo antiguo* ('Collection of little melodies written in old-fashioned style') and is set to a text by Fernando Periquet. In the song a woman celebrates her man who, while lacking traditional good looks, is discreet and can keep the secrets shared between them.

Idiomatic translation

VERSE 1

They tell me my man is ugly, it is possible that he might be,
for love is a desire that makes you blind and dizzy,
there are times when I know through love, one doesn't see.

VERSE 2

Moreover, if my man is not a man who stands out for being beautiful and astonishing,
on the other hand, he is discreet and keeps the secret that I entrusted to him,
knowing that he is reliable.

VERSE 3

What is the secret that my man keeps?
It would be indiscreet for me to tell you, it would be no small task to expose
the secrets of a man and his one woman.
He was born in Lavapies. Hey! Hey! He is a man, a man indeed!

Pronunciation – **El majo discreto** [ɛl mɑxɔ diskrɛtɔ]

VERSE 1

Dicen que mi majo es feo,
diθɛn kɛ mi mɑxɔes fɛɔ

Es posible que si que lo sea
ɛs pɔsiβlɛ kɛ si kɛ lɔ sɛa

que amor es deseo que ciega y marea
kɛamor ɛs desɛɔ kɛ θjɛɣa i marɛa

ha tiempo que sé que quien ama no vé.
a tjɛmpɔ kɛ sɛ kɛ kjɛn ama nɔ bɛ

VERSE 2

Mas si no es mi majo un hombre,
mas si nɔɛs mi mɑxɔ un ɔmbrɛ

que por lindo descuelle y asombre
kɛ pɔr lindɔ dɛskwɛʎɛ iasɔmbrɛ

En cambio es discreto y guarda un secreto
ɛn kambjɔɛs diskrɛtɔ i gwɑrðaun sɛkrɛtɔ

que yo posé en el sabiendo que es fiel.
kɛ jɔ pɔsɛ ɛn ɛl saβjɛndɔ kɛ ɛs fjɛl

VERSE 3

¿Cual es el secreto que el majo guardó?
kwal ɛs ɛl sɛkrɛtɔ kɛl mɑxɔ gwarðɔ

Seria indiscreto contarlo yo,
sɛria indiskrɛtɔ kɔntarlɔ jɔ

No poco trabajo costara saber
nɔ pɔkɔ traβɑxɔ kɔstara saβɛr

secretos de un majo con una mujer.
sɛkrɛtɔs dɛun mɑxɔ kɔn una muxɛr

Nació en Lavapies. ¡Eh! Es un majo un majo es.
naθjɔen laβapjɛs ɛ ɛs un mɑxɔun mɑxɔ ɛs

Further notes

* There is no direct English equivalent for 'majo'. It means a handsome or attractive lover.

El majo discreto
The discreet man

Fernando Periquet

Enrique Granados
(1867–1916)

68

En Jerez de la Frontera

In Jerez de la Frontera   Joaquín Rodrigo (1901–99) *Doce canciones españolas No. 10*

Background

The pianist and composer Joaquín Rodrigo was born in Sagunto, and studied in Valencia and Paris. Left blind from a bout of diphtheria at the age of three, he claimed that this misfortune probably led him towards a career in music. Whilst in Paris he met his wife and Manuel de Falla, who became a lifelong friend. Rodrigo and his wife went to work in Germany, returning to Madrid after the Civil War. Showered with awards and made a noble (*Marqués de los jardines de Aranjuez*) by King Juan Carlos I in 1991, he became Manuel de Falla Professor of Music at Madrid University. Rodrigo's compositions are acclaimed throughout Europe, especially in Spain, and he is particularly remembered for his guitar concerto. His style celebrates the character of Spain's folk tradition. 'En Jerez de la Frontera' is a Spanish folksong written in 1951 and comes from the collection *Doce canciones españolas* ('Twelve Spanish Folksongs').

Idiomatic translation

VERSE 1
In Jerez de la Frontera*, there lived an honest miller,
who earned his living from hiring a mill;
but he was married to a girl, lovely as a rose,
so beautiful, that the new magistrate fell in love with her.

VERSE 2
The miller's wife laughed and when the magistrate demanded
that she love him, she said:
'Ooh, you are witty, too generous, too flattering,
also you are a gentleman, but I love my miller.
He is my master'.

Pronunciation – En Jerez de la Frontera [ɛn xɛɾe̯θ dɛ la frɔntɛ̯ra]

En Jerez de la Frontera
ɛn xɛɾe̯θ dɛ la frɔntɛ̯ra

había un molinero honrado,
aßi̯aun   mɔlinɛɾɔnrrạðɔ

que ganaba su sustento
kɛ ganạßa su sustẹntɔ

con un molino alquilado;
kɔn un mɔlinɔalkilạðɔ

pero es casado
pɛɾɔ ɛs kasạðɔ

con una moza
kɔn ụna mɔθa

como una rosa,
kɔmɔuna rɔsa

como es tan bella,
kɔmɔɛs tan bɛʎa

el corregidor nuevo
ɛl kɔrreɣiðɔr nwɛßɔ

prendó d' ella.
prɛndɔ dɛʎa

En Jerez de la Frontera,
ɛn xɛɾe̯θ dɛ la frɔntɛ̯ra

ríese la molinera,
ri̯esɛ la mɔlinɛ̯ra

y al corregidor decía,
i̯al kɔreɣiðɔr dɛθia

que amores le pedía:
kɛ amɔres lɛ pɛðia

'Ay, sois gracioso,
ai sɔi̯s graθi̯ɔsɔ

muy generoso,
mwi xɛnɛrɔ̯sɔ

muy lisonjero,
mwi lisɔnxẹɾɔ

también caballero,
tambi̯ẹn kaßaʎẹɾɔ

mas quiero a mi molinero
mas ki̯eɾɔa mi mɔlinɛ̯ɾɔ

es mi dueño'
ɛs mi dwẹŋɔ

Further notes

The r's in **honrado** and **corregidor** are strongly rolled so do check the CD and pronunciation guide for these, together with the liaisons as marked.

* In Andalucía

En Jerez de la Frontera

In Jerez de la Frontera

Spanish folksong

Joaquín Rodrigo
(1901–99)

33 *spoken text*
34 *piano accompaniment*

Canción de cuna para dormir a un negrito

Lullaby for a little black boy   Xavier Montsalvatge (1912–2002)

Background

The Spanish composer and teacher Montsalvatge was born in Girona. He studied in Barcelona and later taught at the San Jorge Academy and the Conservatoire. His compositions cover a wide range of musical genres but principal works include ballets, operas and orchestral music. Montsalvatge maintained a long-lasting interest in West Indian musical style, believing it had originated in Spain, was then exported to the West Indies and later re-imported. The collection *Cinco Canciones Negras* (Five Black Songs) (1945–49), from which this lullaby comes, seeks to express some of these ideas. The text of this cradle song, by the Uruguayan poet Ildefonso Valdés (1899–1996), hints that the child is the son of a white landowner and a black slave woman, with all the racial and cultural poignancy those circumstances imply.

Idiomatic translation

Ninghe, ninghe, ninghe, such a tiny little kid, little black boy, who doesn't want to fall asleep.
Coconut head, coffee bean, with lovely freckles, with eyes wide open like two windows looking out to sea.
Shut your little eyes, frightened little black boy; the white devil might eat you up.
You're not a slave any more! – and if you sleep a lot, the master of the house promises to buy you
a suit with buttons so that you will be a groom.
Ninghe, ninghe, ninghe, go to sleep little black boy, coconut head, coffee bean.

Pronunciation – Canción de cuna para dormir a un Negrito
[kanθjɔn dɛ kuna para dɔrmir aun neɣritɔ]

Ninghe, ninghe, ninghe, tan chiquitito,
niŋge   niŋge   niŋge   tan tʃikititɔ

el negrito que no quiere dormir.
ɛl neɣritɔ   kɛ   nɔ kjɛre   dɔrmir

Cabeza de coco, grano de café,
kaßɛθa   dɛ   kɔkɔ   granɔ   de kafɛ

con lindas motitas, con ojos grandotes
kɔn   lindas   mɔtitas   kɔn ɔxɔs grandɔtes

como dos ventanas que miran al mar.
kɔmɔ   dɔs bɛntanas   kɛ   miran   al mar

Cierra los ojitos, negrito asustado;
θjɛrra   lɔs ɔxitɔs   neɣritɔasustaðɔ

el mandinga blanco te puede comer.
ɛl mandiŋga blankɔ tɛ pwɛðe kɔmer

!Ya no eres esclavo!
ja   nɔeres   esklaßɔ

y si duermes mucho el señor de casa
i si dwɛrmes mutʃɔ   ɛl seɲɔr dɛ kasa

promete comprar traje con botones
prɔmɛte   kɔmprar   traxe kɔn   bɔtɔnes

para ser un 'groom'.
para sɛr un grum

Ninghe, ninghe, ninghe, duérmete, negrito,
niŋge   niŋge   niŋge   dwɛrmete   neɣritɔ

Further notes

The word **ninghe** is not a traditional Spanish word, so do check the pronunciation guide.

Canción de cuna para dormir a un negrito
Lullaby for a little black boy

35 spoken text

36 piano accompaniment

Ildefonso Pereda Valdés
(1899–1996)

Xavier Montsalvatge
(1912–2002)

Lento (♩ = 48)
a media vos disminuyendo hasta un final casi imperceptible
(*softly, and diminishing imperceptably to the end*)

Key to International Phonetic Alphabet for Italian

Vowels	IPA	English sounds		Italian words
A	[a]	as in a bright 'ah'		caro [karɔ]
E	[ɛ]	open as in 'bed'		bella [bɛl:la]
	[e]	closed (prepare your tongue as if to say 'ee' and say 'ay' without dropping the jaw)		che [ke]
I	[i]	as in 'see' or 'police'		mi [mi], ti [ti]
O	[o]	closed (say 'oh' with lips in a well-rounded position, jaw slightly dropped and no diphthong)		cosi [kozi]
	[ɔ]	open as in 'hot'		oggi [ɔdʒi]
U	[u]	as in 'food' or 'rude'		tu [tu]

(Please check the pronunciation guides carefully for open and closed vowels as Italian spelling does not differentiate these sounds.)

NB: There are no diphthongs in Italian – the vowels are often liaised but nevertheless, clearly delineated.

Semi-Vowels

	[j]	as in 'yard'	piano [pjanɔ]
	[w]	as in 'water'	acqua [ak:kwa]

Consonants

B, F, M and V are pronounced as in English
D, N, T and L are pronounced as in English but with the tip of the tongue in a forward position, just behind the upper front teeth.

C	[tʃ]	as in 'church'	*before e or i*	ciel [tʃel]
C	[k]	as in 'cook'	*before a, o, u*	cor [kɔr]
SC	[ʃ]	as in 'shoe'	*before e or i*	scena [ʃena]
SC	[sk]	as in 'skull'		scala [skala], scherzo [skertsɔ]
G	[dʒ]	as in 'jar'	*before e or i*	giorni [dʒorni]
G	[g]	as in 'good'		largo [largɔ]
P	[p]	as in 'pull'		pace [patʃe]
QU	[kw]	as in 'quick'		quel [kwel]
R	[ɾ]	slightly flipped 'r'	*between two vowels*	caro [karɔ]
R	[r]	trilled/rolled 'r'		ritardando [ritardandɔ]
S	[s]	as in 'so'		subito [subitɔ]
S	[z]	as in 'zoo'		rosa [rɔza]
Z	[ts]	as in 'pets'		grazia [grat:tsja]
Z	[dz]	as in 'adds'		mezzo [med:dzɔ]

Extra Notes

-GLI-	[ʎ]	like 'million'	*(the g is silent)*	consiglio [kɔnsiʎɔ]
-GN-	[ɲ]	like 'new' (ny-oo)	*(the g is silent)*	segno [seɲɔ]
H		is always silent		hanno [an:nɔ]
H		hardens C, G an SC		che [ke], scherzo [skertsɔ]
I		is silent when used to soften C, G, or SC		già [dʒa], lascia [laʃa]

Double consonants

Any double consonants should be emphasized with a slight 'stop' of the vowel before them – as in allegretto [al:legret:tɔ], cessa [tʃɛs:sa]. A single r is lightly flipped. A double rr is strongly rolled.

Word endings

When singing in Italian, final vowels (unless marked with an accent eg: più [pju]) should never be stressed.

Key to International Phonetic Alphabet for German

Vowels	IPA	English Sounds	German Words
A	[aː]	long – as in 'far'	Vater [faːtə]
	[a]	short – as in 'undo'	Mann [man]
E	[eː]	long – no direct English equivalent but exactly the same as French é (prepare your tongue as if to say 'ee' and say 'ay' without dropping the jaw)	jenem [jeːnəm]
	[ɛ]	short – as in 'bed' or 'set'	denn [dɛn]
	[ə]	neutral – as in 'the' or 'again'	deine [dainə]
I	[iː]	long – as in 'see' or 'police'̀	die [diː], ihm [|iːm]
	[ɪ]	short – as in 'sit' or 'bin'	im [|ɪm], ich [|ɪç]
O	[oː]	long (say 'oh' with lips almost as closed as if for 'ooh' and with no diphthong)	froh [froː]
	[ɔ]	short – as in 'hot'	kommt [kɔmt]
U	[uː]	long – as in 'food' or 'rude'	Blumen [bluːmən]
	[ʊ]	short – as in 'put' or 'book'	und [|ʊnt], um [|ʊm]

Modified Vowels

ä	[ɛː]	long – as in 'gate'	Mädchen [mɛːtçən]
	[ɛ]	short – as in 'bed' or German short 'e'	Hände [hɛndə]
ö	[œ]	short – the same sound as 'earth' but shorter	Hölle [hœlə]
	[øː]	long – as above but with lips more closed (the same as French 'deux'	schöne [ʃøːnə]
ü	[yː]	long (say 'ee' with closed lips in an 'oo' shape)	über [|yːbɐ], Frühling [fryːlɪŋ]
	[ʏ]	short (try saying 'it' with closed lips in an 'oo' shape)	Müller [mʏlə]

Dipthongs

ai, ei	[ai]	as in 'aisle' or 'height'	Mai [mai], mein [main]
au	[au]	as in 'house' or 'flower'	Haus [haus], Frau [frau]
äu, eu	[ɔi]	as in 'boy' or 'oil'	bräutigam [brɔitɪgam], neu [nɔi]

As in English, when singing a diphthong, the singer must spend most time on the first of the combined vowels, leaving the second to the last moment before finishing the word or syllable.

Glottal Stop [|]

The slight stopping of the breath and starting the sound (as in 'umbrella') takes place in German before any word beginning with a vowel. The intensity of this is open to artistic interpretation, but it should never be overdone or in danger of injuring the voice.

Consonants

Consonants are pronounced as in English with the following exceptions:

g is always pronounced hard as in 'good' (but see 'Endings' below)		Gold [gɔlt]
h is silent after a vowel, otherwise it is aspirated		Sohn [zoːn], Hand [hant]
j is pronounced as an English 'y' as in 'yes'		jung [jʊŋ]
k is pronounced before 'n' (it is never silent)		Knabe [knaːbə]
r is slightly 'flipped' [ɾ] before a consonant		sterben [ʃtɛrbən]
r is rolled [r] at the beginning of word or after another consonant		Rose [roːzə], Grab [grap]
s before vowels, as in English 'z' (but see below)		sein [zain], Rose [roːzə]
v mostly as in English 'f'		Vater [faːtə]
w as in English 'v'		Wenn [vɛn]
z as in 'cats'		zum [tsʊm], Tanz [tants]

Double consonants and other sounds

ck	[k]	as in 'lock'	Glück [glyːk]
ch	[x]	after a, o, u and au – closest to Scottish 'loch' (place tongue in the position for 'k' and say 'h')	hoch [hɔx], nach [nax]
ch	[ç]	after e, i, ä, eu or a consonant as in (whispered) 'yes' (place tongue in the position for 'ee' and say 'h')	ich [|ɪç], nächste [nɛːçstə]
ph	[f]	as in 'telephone'	Phantasie [fantaziː]

pf	[pf]	both letters sounded	Pfeil [pfa͟il]
qu	[kv]	sounds like English 'kv ...'	Qual [kva͟ːl]
ß	[s]	as in 'ki<u>ss</u>'	Kuß [kʊs]
sch	[ʃ]	as in English '<u>sh</u>ip'	schöne [ʃø͟ːnə]
sp, st	[ʃp, ʃt]	sounds like English 'sht' or 'shp' *at the beginning of a word, or after a prefix*	Spiel [ʃpiːl], still [ʃtɪl] erstanden [‖ɛɐ̯ʃtandən]
-ng	[ŋ]	as in 'si<u>ng</u>'	kling [klɪŋ]

Note: Unlike Italian, where double consonants are marked, in German, they are treated as single consonants unless the need to express the word more imaginatively leads to emphasizing them (and this would be equally true of single consonants also).

Endings of words/prefixes/word elements

-er	[ɐ]	as in 'sist<u>er</u>'	vater [fa͟ːtɐ]
-r	[ɐ]	usually not pronounced (but check IPA in songs for exceptions)	nur [nu͟ːɐ̯], vor [fo͟ːɐ̯]
-en	[ən]	as in 'gard<u>en</u>'	denken [de͟ŋkən]
b		at the end of a word sounds 'p'	Lieb [li͟ːp]
d		at the end of a word sounds 't'	Lied [li͟ːt], Grund [gru͟nt]
s		at the end of a word as in 'less'	kleines [kla͟inəs]
g		at the end of a word sounds 'k'	Sonntag [zɔ͟ntaːk]
-ig	[ɪç]	as in the German word 'ich'	ewig [‖e͟ːvɪç]

General note

Even though there are many consonants in German, the legato line (as in all singing) is still paramount and consonants need to be quick and crisp.

Key to International Phonetic Alphabet for French

Vowels	IPA	English Sounds	French Words
a	[ɑ]	long – as in 'f<u>a</u>r'	âme [ɑ̱mə]
	[a]	short – as in a bright 'ah'	la [la], caché [kaʃe̱]
e	[e]	long (prepare your tongue as if to say 'ee' and say 'ay' without dropping the jaw)	été [ete̱], et [e]
	[ɛ]	short – as in 'b<u>e</u>d' or 's<u>e</u>t'	est [ɛ], belle [bɛ̱lə]
	[ə]	neutral – as in 't<u>he</u>'	le [lə], que [kə]
i	[i]	long – as in 's<u>ee</u>' or 'pol<u>i</u>ce'	si [si], qui [ki]
o	[o]	long (say 'oh' with lips in a well-rounded position, jaw slightly dropped and no diphthong)	rose [ʀo̱zə], vos [vo]
	[ɔ]	short – as in 'h<u>o</u>t'	comme [kɔ̱mə], col [kɔl]
u	[y]	long (say 'ee' with well-rounded lips in an 'oo' shape)	tu [ty], une [y̱nə]
ou	[u]	long – as in 'f<u>oo</u>d' or 'r<u>u</u>de'	tous [tus], pour [puʀ]
eu	[œ]	open (say '<u>ea</u>rth' and drop the jaw)	leur [lœʀ], coeur [kœʀ]
	[ø]	closed (as above but with lips well-rounded)	deux [dø], feu [fø]

Nasalized Vowels

	[ɑ̃]	long [ɑ] (f<u>a</u>r) nasalized	blanc [blɑ̱̃], semble [sɑ̱̃blə]
	[ɛ̃]	short [æ] (f<u>a</u>t) nasalized	sein [sɛ̃], essaim [esɛ̱̃]
	[õ]	long [o] (<u>oh</u>) nasalized	mon [mõ], ombre [õ̱bʀə]
	[œ̃]	short [œ] (<u>ea</u>rth) nasalized	un [œ̃], parfum [paʀfœ̃]

Although nasal vowels are always followed by an -n or -m in the spelling, these consonants are **not** pronounced either in speech or singing.

Semi Vowels

	[j]	using an English 'y' sound as in 'p<u>ia</u>no'	bien [bjɛ̱̃], ciel [sjɛ̱l]
	[w]	as in 'q<u>ua</u>ck'	moi [mwa], voyant [vwa̱jɑ̃]
	[ɥ]	Try to say [y] (as in 'une') very quickly before the 'i'. It should not sound like a 'w'.	cuivre [kɥi̱vʀə], nuit [nɥi̱]

Consonants

b d f k l m n p t v w y x z

The above consonants are pronounced as in English though in French (as in Italian) there is no explosion of breath with **p, t, k**. Also double consonants are not marked and are spoken or sung as if single.

c	[k]	hard as in 'cook'	*before a,o,u/ending words*	comme [kɔmə], lac [lak]
c/ç	[s]	soft as in 'piece'	*c- before e, i/ç- before a, o, u*	ce [sə], français [fʀɑ̃sɛ]
g	[g]	hard as in 'good'	*before a, o, u*	gauche [goʃə]
	[ʒ]	soft as in 'pleasure'	*before e, i*	age [aʒə]
h		is usually silent		horreur [ɔʀœʀ]
j	[ʒ]	is pronounced as in 'pleasure'		je [ʒə], jardin [ʒaʀdɛ̃]
l	[l]	like an Italian 'forward' 'l' (soft and quick)		
			(but also sometimes silent)	lune [lynə], gentil [ʒɑ̃ti]
qu	[k]	pronounced as a 'k' and without the 'w'		que, [kə] qui [ki]
r	[ʀ]	uvula is vibrated by a vocalised breath against the back of the tongue (see note below)		briser [bʀize]
s	[s]	unvoiced as in 'so'		secret [sekʀɛ]
	[z]	voiced as in 'gaze'	*between two vowels*	cousin [kuzɛ̃]
x	[ks]	as in 'example'		extase [ɛkstɑzə]
	[gs]	as in 'eggs'		examiner [ɛgzamine]
	[z]		*in a liaison*	deux‿amis [dø(z)ami]
		silent as a final consonant	*no liaison*	deux [dø], yeux [jø]

Other Sounds

-ai	[e]	closed 'e' at the end of a word	aimerai [ɛməʀe]
-ais/-ait/-aient	[ɛ]	open 'e' at the end of a word (verb endings)	mais (mɛ), avaient (avɛ)
-au/-eau	[o]	long (say 'oh' with lips in a well-rounded position, jaw slightly dropped and no diphthong)	beau [bo]
ch	[ʃ]	as in 'shoe'	chanter [ʃɑ̃te]
-ail	[aj]	as in English 'eye' (with a pronounced 'y')	travail [tʀavaj]
-eil	[ɛj]	as in English 'eh' followed by 'y'	meilleur (mɛjœʀ)
-euil/oeil	[œj]	as in English 'err' followed by 'y'	feuille (fœj), oeil (œj)
-ouille	[uj]	as in English 'ooh' followed by 'y'	mouiller [muje]
-er/ez	[e]	as a word ending	monter (mɔ̃te), assez (ase)
-gn-	[ɲ]	as in 'onion'	ligne (liɲə)
ph	[f]	as in 'telephone'	séraphin (seʀafɛ̃)
th	[t]	pronounced as a 't'	théatre (teatʀə)

Word endings

A final **-e, -es** and the verb ending **-ent** are silent in speech, but in singing are often given a note. These are sung to the neutral [ə] vowel but should never be emphasized and phrased off tastefully wherever possible.

Liaisons

The decision whether or not to join the final consonant (or consonant plus [ə]) to a following word beginning with a vowel is always a thorny one and the academic rules are complex. Contemporary tastes are always evolving and liaisons are used increasingly less frequently. In this volume, the IPA liaisons will be shown in brackets and should be executed gently and without too much emphasis.

Vowel harmonisations

There are occasions in French where, despite pronunciation rules, vowels are harmonised within a verb. Please check the IPA guide carefully for each song and listen carefully to the CD.

Rolling the 'r' in French

In classical singing, it has been considered good taste to pronounce the rolled 'r' in the Italian style (i.e. with the tip of the tongue in a forward position). Contemporary tastes, however, seem to be moving towards the traditional uvular 'r', even in classical song and opera. In this guide, we recommend the uvular 'r' [ʀ]. In French Baroque repertoire, however, a rolled Italian 'r' would still be considered stylistic.

Key to International Phonetic Alphabet for Spanish

Vowels	IPA	English sounds		Spanish words
a	[a]	as in a bright 'ah'		tan [tan]
e	[ɛ]	open as in 'b<u>e</u>d'		que [kɛ], es [ɛs]
i	[i]	as in 's<u>ea</u>t' or 's<u>ee</u>'		negrito [nɛɣritɔ], si [si]
o	[ɔ]	open as in 'h<u>o</u>t'		ojitos [ɔxitɔs]
u	[u]	as in 'f<u>oo</u>d' or 'r<u>u</u>de'		una [una]
y	[i]	as in '<u>ee</u>' *(only when standing alone as a word)*		y [i]

Semi-Vowels

i, y	[j]	as in '<u>y</u>ard'		bien [bjɛn], yunta [junta]
u	[w]	as in 'ac<u>qua</u>'		cual [kwal]

Diphthongs

ai, ay	[ai]	as in '<u>ai</u>sle'		donaire [dɔnairɛ]
au	[au]	as in 'h<u>ou</u>se'		Laureola [laurɛɔla]
ei, ey	[ɛi]	as in 'th<u>ey</u>'		buey [buɛi]
eu	[ɔi]	as in 'b<u>oy</u>' or '<u>oil</u>'		estoy [ɛstɔi]

Consonants

f k l m n p t

The above consonants are pronounced as in English though softer and not as crisp.

b	[b]	as in 'boy'	*(see notes on v below)*	bomba [bɔmba]
	[ß]		*(see notes on v below)*	labor [laßɔr]
c	[k]	as in '<u>c</u>ook'		casa [kasa]
ce, ci	[θɛ, θi]	as in '<u>th</u>in'	*before* e *or* i	cierra [θjɛrra]
ch	[tʃ]	as in '<u>ch</u>ur<u>ch</u>'		chiquitito [tʃikititɔ]
d	[d]	as in '<u>d</u>ad' *at the beginning of a word or after* l *or* n		dos [dɔs]
	[ð]	as in '<u>th</u>e'	*in any other position*	puede [pwɛðɛ]
g	[g]	as in '<u>g</u>ood' *if at the beginning of a word before* a, o *or* u, *or after* n		guarda [gwarða]
	[ɣ]	a softer [g]	*in any other position*	ciega [θjɛɣa]
ge, gi	[x]	as in Scottish 'lo<u>ch</u>'	*before* e *or* i	gente [xɛntɛ]
h		silent in Spanish		hombre [ɔmbrɛ]
j	[x]	as in Scottish 'lo<u>ch</u>'		majo [maxɔ]
ll	[ʎ]	as in 'mi<u>lli</u>on'		llamar [ʎamar]
ñ	[ɲ]	as in 'o<u>ni</u>on'		niño [niɲɔ]
qu	[k]	as in English 'k'	*before* e *or* i	que [kɛ]
r, rr	[r]	trilled/rolled 'r' *(always pronounced in Spanish)*		grano [granɔ]
s	[s]	as in '<u>s</u>o'		ojos [ɔxɔs], si [si]
	[z]	as in '<u>z</u>oo'	*before* b,d, g l, m *or* n	rasgar [razgar]
v	[b]	as in '<u>b</u>oy' *at the beginning of a word or after* m *or* n		ventanas[bɛntanas]
	[ß]	lips prepared as if to pronounce 'b' but not meeting		esclavo [ɛsklaßɔ]
z	[θ]	as in '<u>th</u>in'		cabeza [kaßɛθa]
x	[ks]	as in 'to<u>x</u>in'		tóxico [tɔksikɔ]
	[s]	as in 's'		
		informal Spanish or at the beginning of a word		xenophobia [sɛnɔfɔßia]